T0314558

Don't Waste Your Turkey

Emily Gussin

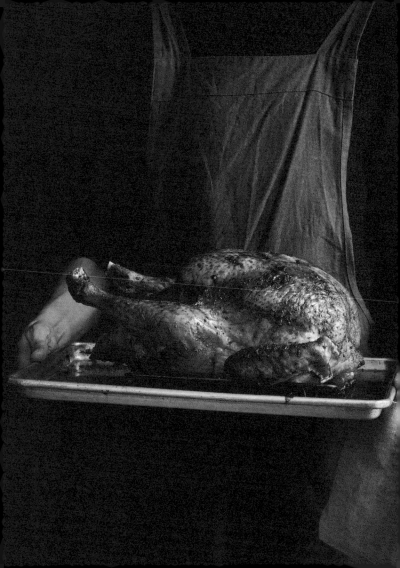

Don't Waste Your TURKEY

Emily Gussin

Innovative recipes
for your festive leftovers

murdoch books
London | Sydney

Contents

Introduction

Leftovers are one of my favourite types of meals, and I hope the recipes in this small book will inspire you to embrace them as an exciting proposition, too.

There is something about opening the fridge and working out what weird and wonderful combinations of food you have to use up that feels fun and frivolous. Creating a fridge-raid dinner you'll never be able to repeat exactly again is both whimsical and freeing.

Boxing Day

In the UK, Boxing Day leftovers are almost as celebrated as the main event Christmas dinner. We love to compile the biggest sandwiches of the year, adding layers of meat, stuffing and trimmings from the day before. As a recipe developer for food magazines, I've spent years looking at the best ways to use up those delicious ingredients cooked for Christmas – each year trying to come up with something more innovative and appealing than the last! It's a challenge I relish.

Turkey traditions

Turkey is quite unique in being synonymous with a specific time of year and, in particular, two festivals: Thanksgiving and Christmas. While it shares similarities with other poultry, it's understandable that if you cook turkey only once a year, you're not going to feel like an expert when doing so. It's also an incredibly big bird and has been bred to grow larger over the last few decades. It makes a spectacular centrepiece for your festive table, but can induce fear in the hearts of the cooks tasked with preparing it. The main reason for this is striking the balance between cooking the bird all the way through and not drying it out, which is tricky but not impossible.

Tried-and-tested techniques

My recipe for a Whole Roast Turkey (page 15) uses a few simple techniques to make sure the meat is tender and juicy. Hopefully this level of detail will give you the results you're looking for.

The other option is to cook the turkey in sections. The white meat of a turkey crown needs to be kept moist (so a faster roast at a higher temperature is ideal), while the dark meat of the legs and wings is very different (and best cooked low and slow until tender enough to pull from the bone). Understandably, it is increasingly popular to buy turkey crowns or rolled joints, as they are much easier to cook, but the problem with this is the wastage. In the UK, approximately 10 million turkeys are sold at Christmas and around 70 per cent of those are sold without the legs. If the crown only is used, what do the farmers do with those millions of legs? Especially in the short time they are all likely to be eaten. This is why I urge you to buy a whole turkey and either joint it yourself (there's a step-by-step guide on page 10) or ask your butcher to do it for you. Leg meat is less popular, as it can be stringy if cooked badly, but I promise you it is meltingly tender and full of flavour when cooked right.

Using this book

This book is divided into three sections. In the From Scratch chapter, I share multiple ways to cook turkey, and cover every bit of it – the legs, wings, breast meat and the whole bird. Leftovers is the largest chapter and is self-explanatory really – once you've got the cooked meat, there's an incredible variety of things you can do with it. The sandwich ideas are here, along with the curry and pie recipes you would expect, but I have also included fried rice, pizza, salads and many more options. I've also included other foods you're likely to have left over after a festive meal, whether that's the scrapings of a jar of cranberry sauce or some braised red cabbage. It's useful to note here that you can freeze cooked turkey, in portions, for up to 3 months, so you don't have to eat it all within a week. The Extras chapter includes all the things often forgotten, but invariably the most delicious, such as using up the turkey fat left in the roasting tin, making the most of the giblets (often sold with the bird) and a recipe for perfect crispy skin.

Avoiding food waste

Our food system is massively under pressure and this has a direct impact on climate change. We are all aware that eating less and better quality meat is incredibly important for the future of our planet. With this in mind, having turkey once or twice a year for a special occasion is a valid option, even if you're trying to cut back on eating meat. The most important thing is to buy the best quality you can, ensuring the turkey is free-range and ideally produced as part of a regenerative farming system – and then use every little bit of it.

How to
Joint a Turkey

Breaking the turkey down into different portions means you can cook each cut in the best way possible. Start by wiping the turkey down so holding onto it is easier, then follow the instructions here.

// Step 1. Sit the turkey on your board breast-side down. Locate the wing joints at the front of the breast and make a cut with a small sharp knife. Pull the wing back to pop the joint open, then cut between the body and wing to remove it.

// Step 2. With the turkey breast-side up, pull both legs outwards. Use a small sharp knife to cut the skin between the thigh and body to release the leg. Pull the leg back with a little force to pop out the leg joint. Cut along from the backbone to remove the leg.

// Step 3. Sit the crown upright and use a large sharp knife to cut through the ribs, down to the base of the bird (you can also use kitchen scissors to do this, one side at a time). Pull the backbone back to pop out the neck joint, then use a small sharp knife to trim around it and remove the backbone from the crown.

// Step 4. If you'd prefer to remove the breasts from the crown, use a long sharp knife to cut along the breast bone. Slice along, moving down a little more each time, to remove the breast meat slowly from the carcass.

From
SCRATCH

Whole roast turkey

This is my ultimate roast turkey recipe. If you're roasting the whole bird, there are a few key things to do to ensure you cook the legs until meltingly tender, while keeping the breast juicy and the skin crisp: brining the turkey overnight helps lock in moisture, butter under the skin of the breast provides a protective layer, and a V-shaped rack on a lipped baking tray helps the legs cook gently. There's no basting required, just a rich and sticky brown-sugar glaze for a stunning glossy finish.

Serves 12–14

6–6.5-kg (13–14-lb) turkey
4 tbsp flaky sea salt
1 tbsp baking powder
2 tbsp dark brown soft sugar

250g (9oz) salted butter, at room temperature
1 tbsp cider vinegar
4 garlic cloves, crushed
2 tsp Worcestershire sauce

V-shaped rack and lipped baking tray

The day before you want to roast the turkey, remove the giblets, neck and wing tips from the turkey (reserve these for stock or Roasting Tin Turkey Gravy, page 93). Use a small sharp knife to remove the wishbone to make it easier to carve later.

Recipe continues overleaf.

Mix together the salt, baking powder and
1 tablespoon sugar, and rub it all over the turkey,
as well as sprinkling some inside the cavity. Sit
the turkey on the V-shaped rack set on the lipped
baking tray, then put in the fridge, uncovered, for
24 hours.

Remove the turkey from the fridge 2 hours
before you plan to start cooking it and wipe any
liquid from the tray.

About 30 minutes before the turkey is due to go
into the oven, preheat the oven to 250°C (230°C
fan/500°F/Gas 9).

Meanwhile, rub one-third of the butter under the
skin of the turkey breast and another third all
over the outside of the turkey.

For the glaze, heat the remaining butter in a
small pan with the remaining 1 tablespoon sugar,
the vinegar, garlic and Worcestershire sauce.
Bring to a simmer over a medium heat and
bubble for 2 minutes to thicken a little. Remove
from the heat and set aside for later.

Add vegetables and herbs to the tray under the rack for extra flavour for the Roasting Tin Turkey Gravy (page 93).

If your turkey is 5-6kg (11-13lb) it will need roughly 15 minutes less cooking time; if it is 4-5kg (8¾-10lb) it will need around 30 minutes less.

Add a small mugful of water to the baking tray, put the turkey in the oven and reduce the temperature to 160°C (140°C fan/325°F/Gas 3). Roast for 2½–3 hours, brushing the turkey with the glaze every hour, until the thickest part of the breast registers 72°C (162°F) on a probe thermometer (it should then reach 74°C/165°F after resting).

Transfer the turkey to a board and leave to rest for 45 minutes–1 hour before carving (don't cover it with foil otherwise the skin will turn soft). Use the juices in the baking tray to make Roasting Tin Turkey Gravy (page 93).

From Scratch

How to
Carve a Turkey

Before roasting a whole turkey, it is best to remove the wishbone with a small sharp knife to make it easier to carve later. Once cooked and rested, it is time to carve as follows.

// Step 1. Sit the rested turkey on a board with the legs closest to you. Run a carving knife through the skin between the crown and leg to release it. Press the leg out to pop out the joint, then continue slicing to remove the leg. Repeat with the other leg.

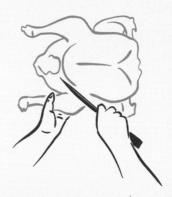

// Step 2. You can separate the thighs from the drumsticks by pulling the legs open, then slicing between the joint. Or, leave whole and shred the meat using two forks or your hands to flake it off the bone, removing the bone-like tendons. You can also do this with the wings.

// Step 3. Remove the whole turkey breasts from the carcass by cutting along the breast bone with long strokes, slowly moving further down, following the shape of the ribs, until you've removed the breast on each side.

// Step 4. Cut the breast across the grain to give thick slices. Keep the carcass for stock (page 88).

Confit turkey legs

Gently cooked in oil, this recipe is inspired by the classic French duck dish. The confit process makes the turkey meat meltingly tender.

Serves 4-6

2 tbsp black
   peppercorns
1 tbsp caraway seeds
4 tbsp flaky sea salt
2 turkey legs

2 garlic bulbs, halved
   horizontally
2 bay leaves
3 sprigs rosemary
about 1 litre (1¾ pints)
   olive oil

Toast the peppercorns and caraway seeds in a dry frying pan for a few minutes until fragrant. Lightly crush with a pestle and mortar, then stir in the salt.

Put the turkey legs in a container with a lid and rub the salt mixture over. Seal the lid and leave to sit at room temperature for 2 hours (or chill for up to 24 hours) to dry brine.

Preheat the oven to 160°C (140°C fan/325°F/Gas 3).

Brush the salt brine off the turkey legs and transfer them to a tight-fitting flameproof casserole dish with a lid. Nestle the garlic, bay and rosemary around the legs, then add enough oil so that everything is submerged.

Keep the oil left over from confiting the turkey to use in other dishes. Strain it through a fine sieve (strainer), then keep in an airtight container in the fridge for up to 6 months.

Place the casserole dish over a medium heat, bring to a simmer, then cover with the lid and transfer to the oven. Bake for 2½–3 hours until the meat is very tender and falls off the bone easily.

Enjoy straight away or keep the meat in the fat in a container in the fridge for up to 2 weeks. You can also squeeze out the garlic cloves to enjoy alongside.

Harissa turkey skewers

Warmly spiced with harissa paste, these skewers are great for offcuts of turkey breast or thigh meat. Cutting the meat thinly – or bashing it out – makes it quick to cook, so it's really juicy. Serve with a cous cous salad or in wraps.

Serves 2

300g (10½oz) turkey breast
50g (1¾oz) natural yogurt
2 tbsp rose harissa

fresh juice of ½ lemon
1 tbsp olive oil
salt and black pepper

metal or soaked bamboo skewers

Cut the turkey into slices about 5mm (¼ inch) thick, or put the meat between two sheets of baking paper and use a rolling pin to bash it out to an even thickness of about 5mm (¼ inch). Season the turkey with salt and pepper.

In a bowl, stir together the yogurt, harissa and lemon juice. Add the turkey and coat it in the yogurt mixture. Leave to marinate for 30 minutes at room temperature (or 2 hours in the fridge).

Heat the grill (broiler) to high.

These cook beautifully on a barbecue, too.

Thread the marinated turkey onto skewers so that it folds over on itself, giving a ribbon effect along the skewer.

Place the turkey skewers on a wire rack set over a lipped baking tray, then drizzle with the oil. Grill (broil) for 2–3 minutes on each side until golden and cooked through.

Buffalo hot wings

Spicy wings, supersized! These take a bit more time than the chicken version, but are totally worth it. Juicy on the inside, crisp on the outside, and coated in buttery hot sauce.

Serves 2

2 turkey wings
1 tbsp flaky sea salt
½ tsp baking powder
1 tsp freshly ground
  black pepper

½ tsp onion powder
40g (1½oz) unsalted
  butter
3 tbsp buffalo hot sauce
½ tsp smoked paprika
2 tsp cider vinegar

Preheat the oven to 160°C (140°C fan/325°F/Gas 3). Sit a wire rack onto a lipped baking tray.

Divide the turkey wings into flats and drumettes, using a small sharp knife to cut between the joints.

In a large bowl, stir together the salt, baking powder, black pepper and onion powder. Pat the wings dry, then toss in the salt mixture to coat evenly.

Place the wings on the rack and bake for 1 hour.

Leave the wing tips attached or remove them to use for stock or gravy another time.

Increase the oven to 220°C (200°C fan/425°F/ Gas 7) and bake for 30 minutes more, turning halfway, until the wings are golden and crisp.

While they finish roasting, combine the butter, hot sauce, paprika and vinegar in a small pan. Cook over a medium heat for a few minutes until the butter has melted and thickened into a smooth sauce.

Toss the cooked wings in the sauce and serve straight away.

Turkey, barley and white bean stew

A comforting, wholesome stew for chilly days. It's subtly flavoured with caraway, garlic and parsley, but could be drizzled with chilli oil for a lick of heat.

Serves 4

1 tbsp olive oil
1 large red onion, chopped
2 carrots, chopped
2 celery stems, chopped
1 large leek, sliced
1 tsp caraway seeds
2 garlic cloves, sliced
handful of parsley, stems finely chopped, leaves roughly chopped

1kg (2lb 4oz) turkey legs, drumsticks or thigh joints
150g (5¼oz) pearl barley
325-g (11-oz) jar or 400-g (14-oz) can white beans, drained
salt and black pepper

Heat the oil in a large flameproof casserole dish over a medium heat. Add the onion, carrots, celery and leek with a good pinch of salt and sauté for 15 minutes until light golden and softening.

Stir in the caraway seeds, garlic and parsley stems.

Remove the skin from the turkey (use it to make Crispy Turkey Skin Crackling, page 103) then add to the pan along with 1.5 litres (2²/₃ pints) water. Bring to the boil, then cover with a lid, reduce the heat and simmer gently for 45 minutes.

Add the barley, cover with the lid and cook for 40 minutes more.

Lift the turkey out of the stew onto a board and tip the beans into the pan. Continue to cook while you shred the meat. Use two forks to shred the turkey, then return this to the pan. Season with salt and pepper and stir through the parsley leaves to serve.

Bacon-wrapped turkey in mustard sauce

Parcels of turkey breast wrapped in salty bacon are delicious in a punchy, silky double-mustard sauce. Serve them with mashed potatoes or steamed rice and greens.

Serves 4

8 outdoor-reared streaky bacon rashers
4 x 150-g (5¼-oz) skinless turkey breast fillets
1 tbsp olive oil
1 bay leaf
1 tbsp plain (all-purpose) flour

200ml (7fl oz) white wine
400ml (14fl oz) Turkey Stock (page 88) or chicken stock
1½ tbsp wholegrain mustard
2 tsp Dijon mustard
100ml (3½fl oz) double (heavy) cream
chopped parsley, to serve

Preheat the oven to 220°C (200°C fan/425°F/Gas 7).

Put the bacon on a board and use the edge of a knife to stretch it gently. Wrap two pieces of bacon around each piece of turkey. Place the wrapped fillets in a flameproof roasting dish or ovenproof pan, drizzle with the oil and tuck a bay leaf underneath.

Recipe continues overleaf.

Roast for 20–25 minutes until the turkey is cooked through.

Lift the turkey out onto a plate to rest. Place the pan over a medium heat and add the flour. Stir to cook out for a few minutes, then add the wine and bubble to reduce by half. Gradually add the stock, then continue to cook until it thickens. Stir in the wholegrain and Dijon mustards and the cream and cook for 2 minutes.

Serve the bacon-wrapped turkey with the mustard sauce and the parsley scattered over.

Turkey tenders

Crisp Parmesan and panko-coated turkey strips are the perfect finger food, or great for piling into a burger bun.

Serves 2

100g (3½oz) yogurt
½ tsp Dijon mustard
½ tsp honey
400g (14oz) turkey
    breast, cut into strips
    2.5cm (1 inch) wide
2 tbsp plain (all-
    purpose) flour

1 tsp smoked paprika
1 tsp onion granules
2 free-range eggs
50g (1¾oz) panko
    breadcrumbs
20g (¾oz) Parmesan,
    finely grated
olive oil, for frying
salt

Mix the yogurt, mustard and honey in a bowl, then add the turkey strips. Leave to marinate for 20–30 minutes at room temperature.

Put the flour, paprika, onion granules and a pinch of salt in a bowl and stir. In another bowl, lightly beat the eggs. In a third bowl, mix the breadcrumbs and Parmesan. Lift a strip of turkey out of the marinade, allow the excess to drip off, then coat in the flour, then the egg and then the breadcrumbs. Repeat with all of the turkey.

Heat a frying pan with 1cm (½ inch) of oil over a medium heat. Test it's ready by dropping in a breadcrumb – you want it to sizzle. Add the turkey strips (in batches if needed) and cook for about 6 minutes on each side until golden and cooked through. Keep warm in a low oven if doing this in batches.

Turkey au vin

A twist on the hearty classic French casserole, this recipe braises turkey legs instead of chicken in lardons, mushrooms and red wine.

Serves 4-6

2 turkey legs
1 tbsp olive oil
150g (5¼oz) bacon
  lardons
12 small shallots, peeled
4 garlic cloves, crushed
1 tbsp concentrated
  tomato purée
1 bay leaf
3 tbsp plain (all-
  purpose) flour
750ml (1¼ pints) robust
  red wine
250ml (9fl oz) Turkey
  Stock (page 88) or
  chicken stock
200g (7oz) button
  mushrooms
salt and black pepper

Season the turkey legs. Heat the olive oil in a large lidded flame-proof casserole dish over a medium–high heat. Add the legs and cook for 10 minutes or until browned all over. Transfer to a plate. Scoop out the fat with a spoon, leaving 1 tablespoon in the pan.

Add the lardons and shallots to the pan and cook for about 6 minutes until golden. Add the garlic, followed by the tomato purée and bay leaf. Cook for about a minute, then stir in the flour. Cook for another minute, then pour in the wine and stock. Bring to a simmer, then add the mushrooms and the turkey legs.

Recipe continues overleaf.

Cover and bubble gently for 1½ hours, then
remove the lid and cook for another 30 minutes
until the turkey is very tender.

Remove the legs from the pan and shred the
meat. Meanwhile, increase the heat to high to
thicken the sauce. Season to taste, add the meat
back to the sauce and serve.

Roast turkey legs with grapes

Grapes are delicious roasted in the juices of turkey legs, adding a burst of sweetness to the tender slow-cooked meat. Serve with potatoes or crusty bread.

Serves 4

2 turkey legs
100ml (3½fl oz) white wine
200ml (7fl oz) Turkey Stock (page 88) or chicken stock
8 garlic cloves
500g (1lb 2oz) red grapes
small handful of tarragon leaves
salt and black pepper

Get the turkey legs out of the fridge 30 minutes before cooking them. Season well with salt. Preheat the oven to 220°C (200°C fan/425°F/Gas 7).

Sit the turkey in a roasting tin and roast for 30 minutes. Baste the legs, then carefully pour most of the fat collected in the roasting tin into a bowl (keep for Whipped Turkey Butter, page 95, or Turkey Fat Mayonnaise, page 90). Add the wine, stock and garlic cloves to the roasting tin. Nestle the grapes around the turkey.

Reduce the oven temperature to 160°C (140°C fan/325°F/Gas 3) and cook for 1 hour 15 minutes until the meat is tender enough to shred with a fork. Season, scatter over the tarragon and serve.

Bacon-latticed turkey crown

Layering a turkey crown with strips of bacon looks fantastic but also helps lock in moisture, so you have really juicy meat.

Serves 8–10

- 2 tbsp flaky sea salt
- 2 tsp baking powder
- 2 sprigs rosemary, leaves finely chopped
- 2 tsp caster (superfine) sugar
- 4-kg (9-lb) turkey crown
- 2 carrots, halved lengthways
- 1 large onion, cut into wedges
- 2 thick celery sticks or 1 leek, halved lengthways
- 300g (10½oz) outdoor-reared streaky bacon
- 1 garlic bulb, halved widthways
- 300ml (10½fl oz) Turkey Stock (page 88) or chicken stock

The day before you want to roast the turkey crown, mix together the salt, baking powder, rosemary and sugar, and rub it all over the turkey. Sit the turkey in a roasting tin, then put in the fridge, uncovered, for 24 hours to dry brine.

Remove the turkey from the fridge 1 hour before you plan to start cooking it and lift it onto a board. Wipe any liquid from the tin and arrange the vegetables inside to create a trivet on which the turkey will sit. Lay the bacon over the turkey crown in a crisscross pattern to cover the surface.

Preheat the oven to 200°C (180°C fan/400°F/ Gas 6).

Put the garlic in the roasting tin and pour in the stock (to the side of the turkey). Roast for 1 hour 20 minutes–1 hour 45 minutes, basting the crown every 45 minutes, until the thickest part of the breast registers 74°C (165°F) on a probe thermometer.

Transfer to a board to rest, loosely tented with foil, for 45 minutes–1 hour while you make Roasting Tin Turkey Gravy (page 93) with the contents of the roasting tin.

Slow-roast turkey legs on potatoes

Slow cooking the turkey legs on top of a tin of boulangère-style sliced potatoes and celeriac, means the fat drips into them, making them luxuriously rich.

Serves 4

2 turkey legs
400g (14oz) King Edward or Maris Piper potatoes
350g (12oz) celeriac (celery root)
1 onion

handful of sage leaves, sliced
300ml (10½fl oz) Turkey Stock (page 88) or chicken stock
salt and black pepper

20 x 30-cm (8 x 12-inch) oven dish

Get the turkey legs out of the fridge 30 minutes before cooking them and season well with salt. Preheat the oven to 200°C (180°C fan/400°F/Gas 6).

Cut the potatoes, celeriac and onion into thin slices. Layer them up in the oven dish, adding the sage and seasoning with salt and pepper as you go. Pour over the stock, then sit the turkey legs on top. Roast for 45 minutes.

Reduce the oven temperature to 160°C (140°C fan/325°F/Gas 3) and cook for 45 minutes–1 hour until the meat is tender enough to pull apart with a fork.

Ginger and garlic poached turkey with rice

Inspired by Hainanese chicken and rice, this simple and aromatic poached turkey is served with rice cooked in the poaching liquid. Truly soul nourishing.

Serves 4

1.5kg (3¼lb) skin-on turkey pieces (a mixture of drumsticks, thigh portions and breast)
40g (1½oz) ginger
8 garlic cloves
4 spring onions (scallions), greens and whites separated, sliced

1 star anise
1 tsp fine sea salt
½ tsp black peppercorns
1 tbsp sesame oil
300g (10½oz) jasmine rice, rinsed
kecap manis, to serve
chilli-garlic sauce, to serve
salt

Remove the turkey from the fridge 1 hour before cooking. Remove any large pieces of fat from the turkey, without removing the skin, and set aside.

Recipe continues overleaf.

Fill a large pan with 1.5 litres (2⅔ pints) water and bring to the boil. Roughly chop half the ginger and add to the pan with half of the garlic, the spring onion whites, the star anise, salt and peppercorns. Add the drumstick and thigh portions and simmer gently for 1½ hours, adding any breast portions for the final 30 minutes.

When there's 10 minutes of cooking time left, put the reserved fat pieces in a medium saucepan over a low–medium heat and cook gently to render out the fat.

Prepare an ice-water bath.

Once the turkey is cooked, use tongs to transfer it to the ice-water bath and leave for 10 minutes to cool quickly. Reserve the poaching liquid.

Once cool, lift the turkey onto a wire rack set over a tray and coat with the sesame oil. Set aside while you prepare everything else.

Finely grate the remaining ginger and garlic and add this to the rendered fat. Cook for 2 minutes, then stir in the rice. Cook for a few minutes, stirring, until coated. Add 600ml (1 pint) of the turkey poaching liquid and a good pinch of salt, cover and bring to the boil. Simmer for 9 minutes, then remove from the heat without touching the lid. Set aside to steam with the lid on for 10 minutes.

While the rice cooks, remove the aromatics from the remaining poaching liquid, then boil to reduce the liquid by two-thirds. Keep warm over a low heat.

Serve the rice and room-temperature turkey sprinkled with the spring onion greens, and with some kecap manis and chilli-garlic sauce on the side for dipping. Serve the poaching broth in a bowl on the side for spooning over the dish.

Turkey meatballs

Cooked in a sundried tomato and passata sauce, these meatballs are a great way to use turkey breast meat. The mixture includes soaked bread and cream cheese to give them a light, juicy texture.

Serves 4

1 slice wholemeal bread, about 50g (1¾oz)
500g (1lb 2oz) turkey breast, roughly chopped
1 onion, finely chopped
2 garlic cloves, crushed
50g (1¾oz) cream cheese
60g (2oz) sundried tomatoes from a jar, plus 2 tbsp of the oil
700g (1½lb) tomato passata (puréed tomatoes)
salt and black pepper

Put the bread in a shallow bowl and cover with water. Leave to soak for 5 minutes.

Meanwhile, put the turkey and onion in a food processor and whizz to a coarse paste. Drain the bread, squeeze out some of the water, then tear into the food processor. Add half the garlic, the cream cheese and season with salt and pepper. Whizz again until all combined.

Use wet hands to shape the mixture into 16 meatballs.

Heat the oil from the sundried tomatoes in a large frying pan over a medium–high heat. Add the meatballs and cook for 6–8 minutes until golden all over.

From Scratch

You can also use turkey mince (ground turkey) to make these meatballs. Simply mix all the ingredients in a bowl rather than whizzing in a food processor.

Chop the sundried tomatoes and add these to the pan with the rest of the garlic. Cook for 1 minute, then stir in the passata.

Bring to a simmer, cover with a lid and bubble gently for 15 minutes, stirring halfway, until the meatballs have cooked through. Season to taste and serve with spaghetti or potatoes.

With
LEFTOVERS

Turkey slaw sandwich

A quick, crunchy, juicy slaw is the perfect partner for tender roast turkey in a sandwich.

Serves 4

2 carrots
8 radishes
2 spring onions
  (scallions)
4 tbsp mayonnaise or
  Turkey Fat
  Mayonnaise (page 90)

3 tbsp crème fraîche
  (or sour cream)
1 tsp white wine vinegar
butter, for spreading
8 slices bread
300g (10½oz) left-over
  turkey, ideally breast,
  at room temperature
salt and black pepper

Coarsely grate the carrot and finely slice the radishes and spring onions. Tumble together in a bowl then add the mayo, crème fraîche and vinegar. Season with salt and pepper.

Butter the bread, then pile up the slaw and turkey on four of the slices. Top with the remaining bread slices and enjoy.

Brie, turkey and caramelised onion toastie

Creamy Brie and tangy caramelised onion chutney are delicious sandwiched around left-over turkey in a gooey, hot toastie.

Serves 2

butter, for spreading
4 slices bread
3 tbsp caramelised
   onion chutney

150g (5¼oz) left-over
   turkey, at room
   temperature
100g (3½oz) Brie,
   chopped

Spread some butter on one side of the slices of bread. Turn over two of the slices and spread the onion chutney on the other side, then top with the turkey and Brie. Place the other slices on top, butter-side up.

Heat a large frying pan or flat griddle pan over a medium heat. Add the toastie, then top with a baking tray or another pan and weigh down with something heavy. Cook for 3–4 minutes, until golden and toasted, then flip and repeat on the other side, until crisp on the outside and melted in the middle.

Turkey and cranberry sandwich

Using up your roast dinner leftovers in a sandwich can't be beaten. I've mixed the roast turkey with capers for a little brightness, added shredded greens for crunch and included cranberry sauce for a tangy finish.

Serves 2

150g (5¼oz) left-over turkey, cut into strips
2 tbsp mayonnaise or Turkey Fat Mayonnaise (page 90)
1 tsp capers, chopped

100g (3½oz) left-over roasted root veg (carrots, parsnips, sweet potatoes, etc)
butter, for spreading
4 slices soft bread
2 tbsp cranberry sauce
small handful of shredded sprouts or spinach
salt and black pepper

Get the left-over turkey out of the fridge and allow to come to room temperature for 30 minutes.

Stir the mayonnaise and capers through the turkey and season with salt and pepper. Warm the left-over root veg in a microwave or frying pan.

Pillowy focaccia is a great option for sandwiches in my opinion. Instead of four slices of standard bread, use two squares of focaccia and cut them in half horizontally.

Butter all four slices of bread, then spread the cranberry sauce on two of the slices (one for each sandwich). Top the other slices with the turkey, followed by the root veg and the greens. Sandwich the cranberry sauce-coated slice on top and enjoy.

Kimchi turkey fried rice

Tangy, spicy kimchi cuts through rich turkey meat in this quick and healthy fried rice dinner, topped with a fried egg.

Serves 2

2 tsp vegetable oil, plus extra for frying the eggs

2 spring onions (scallions), greens and whites separated, both thinly sliced

10g (1/3oz) ginger, grated

2 garlic cloves, crushed

100g (3½oz) shredded cabbage or other green veg

1 tbsp gochujang

150g (5¼oz) kimchi

200g (7oz) cooked and cooled jasmine rice

150g (5¼oz) left-over turkey, ideally dark meat, shredded

1 tbsp soy sauce

1 tbsp sesame oil

1 tsp clear honey

2 free-range eggs

Heat the oil in a large wok or frying pan over a medium–high heat. Add the spring onion whites, ginger and garlic to the pan and increase the heat to high. Stir fry for a minute, then add the veg. Cook for another minute or so until wilted, then stir in the gochujang and kimchi.

Recipe continues overleaf.

Add the cooked rice and left-over turkey.
Stir-fry for a few minutes, then add the soy
sauce, sesame oil and honey, and cook for
another minute.

Divide between two bowls, then return the pan
to the heat. Add a little more oil and, once hot,
crack in the eggs. Season and cook the eggs
to your liking, then place one on top of each
portion. Scatter over the spring onion greens
to serve.

Turkey stroganoff

With its origins in 19th-century Russia, stroganoff now comes in many guises. Here, we're adding roast turkey to the creamy sauce, whether you've got breast or dark meat left over.

Serves 2

2 tsp olive oil
1 onion, sliced
¼ tsp paprika
300g (10½oz) mushrooms, sliced
50ml (1¾fl oz) white wine

100ml (3½fl oz) Turkey Stock (page 88) or chicken stock
1 tsp Dijon mustard
150g (5¼oz) crème fraîche
1 tbsp soy sauce
250g (9oz) left-over turkey, cut into chunks
salt

Heat the oil in a large frying pan over a low heat, then add the onion with a pinch of salt and cook gently for about 15 minutes until very soft. Stir in the paprika, then tip the onion onto a plate.

Return the pan to a medium–high heat and add the mushrooms. Fry for 5 minutes until browned all over. Scrape the onions back into the pan. Add the wine and let it bubble to reduce by half.

Add the stock and mustard and bring it back to a simmer. Once bubbling, stir in the crème fraîche and soy sauce until combined and creamy. Add the turkey and cook gently for about 5 minutes until heated through, then season and serve.

Coronation turkey baked potatoes

Lightly spiced with curry powder and sweet with mango chutney, coronation turkey is a great topping for fluffy baked potatoes. Stir some fresh coriander into mint sauce for an easy topping.

Serves 4

4 baking potatoes
8 tbsp mayonnaise
(or Turkey Fat
Mayonnaise, page 90)
1 tbsp mild curry
powder
½ tsp turmeric powder
1 tsp concentrated
tomato purée
2 tbsp mango chutney

200g (7oz) Greek
yogurt
400g (14oz) left-over
turkey, cut into strips
50g (1¾oz) baby
spinach, chopped
handful of coriander
(cilantro), chopped
2 tbsp mint sauce
olive oil, for rubbing
salt and black pepper
salted butter, to serve

Preheat the oven to 220°C (200°C fan/425°F/Gas 7).

Rub a little olive oil over each potato and season with salt. Put them directly on a shelf in the oven and bake for about 50 minutes until the skin is crisp and the potato is soft inside. (To speed things up, you can give them a 10-minute blast in the microwave, followed by 20 minutes in the oven.)

Meanwhile, in a large bowl combine the mayonnaise, curry powder, turmeric, tomato purée, mango chutney and yogurt. Add the turkey, spinach and some of the coriander, and season with salt and pepper.

In a small bowl, stir the rest of the coriander into the mint sauce.

To serve, split open the baked potatoes and add some butter. Divide the coronation turkey filling amongst the four potatoes, then spoon over the mint sauce.

Chickpea, turkey and sweet potato pie

Cumin, paprika and preserved lemon add depth of flavour to sweet potatoes, chickpeas and left-over turkey in this spiced pot pie. It is topped with scrunched up sheets of crisp, butter-coated filo pastry.

Serves 4

2 small or 1 large sweet potato, cut into 3-cm (1¼-inch) chunks
1 tbsp olive oil
1 large onion, sliced
1 large carrot, sliced into rounds
3 garlic cloves, crushed
1 tbsp concentrated tomato purée
400-g (14-oz) jar or can chickpeas (garbanzo beans), including their liquid

1 preserved lemon, flesh removed and rind chopped
1 tsp ground cumin
1 tsp smoked paprika
250g (9oz) left-over turkey
5 sheets filo pastry
40g (1½oz) salted butter, melted
salt and black pepper

20 x 30-cm (8 x 12-inch) baking dish

Preheat the oven to 220°C (200°C fan/425°F/ Gas 7).

Put the sweet potato in a pan of salted water, bring to the boil and simmer for 15 minutes.

Meanwhile, heat the olive oil in a large pan over a medium heat, add the onion and carrot with a pinch of salt and cook for 12 minutes until softening. Stir in the garlic and tomato purée and cook for 1 minute, then add the chickpeas, preserved lemon and spices. Bring to a simmer then stir through the turkey and drained sweet potato. Season with salt and pepper.

Tip the mixture into the baking dish. Unroll the filo pastry sheets on the work surface and brush them with the melted butter. Scrunch them up and arrange them on top of the filling to cover the surface. Drizzle over any remaining butter.

Bake for about 25 minutes until golden.

Blood orange, radicchio and turkey lentil salad

Fragrant blood oranges, bitter radicchio and delicate goat's cheese work brilliantly with roast turkey and lentils in this warm winter salad.

Serves 2

500ml (16fl oz) vegetable stock
150g (5¼oz) dried Puy or green lentils, rinsed
1 blood or blush orange
2 tbsp extra virgin olive oil
1 head radicchio, leaves separated
150g (5¼oz) left-over turkey
2 tsp white wine vinegar
1 tsp honey
50g (1¾oz) goat's cheese
salt and black pepper

Put the stock in a medium saucepan and bring to the boil. Add the lentils, cover and simmer for 30–35 minutes until the lentils are tender. Drain in a colander.

Meanwhile, finely grate the zest of the orange into a large bowl. Top and tail the orange then remove the peel, slicing down it in sections. Cut into slices about 1cm (½ inch) thick.

Reserve the lentil cooking stock to use as the base of a sauce for another dish; it has plenty of flavour.

Heat a large frying pan over a high heat and add ½ tablespoon oil. Fry the orange slices for about 30 seconds on each side until lightly charred, then transfer to a plate. Add the radicchio leaves to the frying pan and cook over a medium heat for about 1 minute, stirring, until softened a little. Add the turkey, season and cook for another minute to warm through.

For the dressing, whisk the remaining 1½ tablespoons oil with the vinegar, honey and orange zest and season to taste.

Toss the dressing through the lentils, radicchio and turkey. Pile the salad onto a serving platter, scatter over the cheese and top with the charred orange slices.

Turkey spinach curry

Curry is a popular way to use up left-over roast turkey. This one is vibrant with plenty of green spinach and the rich red of crushed tomatoes, with a good depth of spice. Serve with steamed rice or chapatis.

Serves 4

1 tbsp ghee or vegetable oil
1 tsp cumin seeds
1 large onion, sliced
2 tbsp ginger garlic paste
2 tsp Kashmiri chilli powder
2 tsp garam masala
1 tsp ground coriander
2 x 400-g (14-oz) cans plum tomatoes
300g (10½oz) left-over turkey, torn into chunks
450g (1lb) baby spinach, roughly chopped
2 tbsp natural (plain) yogurt
salt and black pepper

Heat the ghee in a large frying pan, then add the cumin seeds. Once sizzling, add the onion with a pinch of salt. Cook over a medium heat for 8 minutes.

Add the ginger garlic paste and cook for another minute. Stir through 1 teaspoon chilli powder, 1 teaspoon garam masala and the ground coriander.

Tip the tomatoes into the pan, crushing them with a wooden spoon, then add a splash of water to each can and rinse out into the pan. Bring to a simmer and bubble gently for about 10 minutes until thickened slightly.

Meanwhile, put the turkey in a bowl and toss through the remaining 1 teaspoon chilli powder and 1 teaspoon garam masala, as well as a good pinch of salt. Set aside.

Add the spinach to the pan and cook, covered, over a low–medium heat for 15 minutes.

Stir in the turkey and cook for 5 minutes without the lid. Stir through the yogurt and season to taste, then serve.

Turkey, artichoke, leek and ricotta pizza

With ricotta and mozzarella, this double-cheese white pizza combines turkey with leeks and tinned artichokes. If you have left-over cooked sprouts, parsnips or carrots, you can swap them in instead.

Serves 4

500g (1lb 2oz) strong white flour
1 tsp fine sea salt
7g (¼oz) fast-action dried yeast
250ml (9fl oz) warm water
4 tbsp olive oil, plus extra to serve
1 tsp dried thyme
500g (1lb 2oz) ricotta

1 small leek, thinly sliced
400-g (14-oz) can artichokes, drained and halved
200g (7oz) left-over turkey, torn into chunks
150g (5¼oz) dry mozzarella, torn into chunks
salt and black pepper

In the bowl of a stand mixer fitted with the dough hook, combine the flour, salt and yeast.

Recipe continues overleaf.

In a jug, combine the warm water and olive oil. Pour the liquid into the flour while mixing on a slow speed to combine, then knead the dough at a low–medium speed for about 5 minutes until smooth. Alternatively, knead by hand until smooth. Cover the bowl and leave to rest in a warm place for about 1 hour until the dough has doubled in size.

Preheat the oven to 270°C (250°C fan/520°F/ Gas 10) with two large baking trays inside.

Stir the thyme and a pinch of salt into the ricotta, and get all of the toppings ready.

Cut the rested dough into quarters. Put a large, heavy-based frying pan over a high heat. Take one ball and roll or stretch it out into a rough 15-cm (6-inch) round. Place it in the hot pan so the base starts to cook while you add the toppings. Leaving a 1-cm (½-inch) border, spread over one-quarter of the ricotta, then top with leek, artichokes and turkey. Dot over the mozzarella.

Use a spatula to transfer the pizza to one of the heated baking trays and bake for 6–8 minutes until golden and the base is cooked through. Repeat with the other three pizzas while it cooks. Season and drizzle with extra olive oil to serve.

Chipotle turkey tacos

Earthy, smoky chipotle chilli creates an intense coating for left-over turkey. Paired with zesty radishes quick-pickled in lime juice, you have an easy topping for taco Tuesdays.

Serves 4

1 dried chipotle chilli
2 garlic cloves
400ml (14fl oz) hot Turkey Stock (page 88) or chicken stock
100g (3½oz) radishes, sliced
juice of 2 limes
1 tsp dried oregano
3 tbsp concentrated tomato purée
350g (12oz) left-over turkey, shredded
12 small corn tortillas
2 tbsp sour cream
small handful of coriander (cilantro)
salt

Dry fry the chilli and garlic (peeled but left whole) in a large frying pan for a few minutes on each side until charred. Transfer to a jug with the hot vegetable stock and soak for 10 minutes.

Meanwhile, put the radishes in a bowl with the lime juice, 1 tbsp water and a pinch of salt. Set aside, stirring every now and then.

Whizz the stock mixture, oregano and tomato purée in a blender until smooth. Pour into the pan, add the turkey and simmer for 8 minutes until reduced enough to just coat the turkey.

Toast the tortillas in a dry frying pan and serve the tortillas piled with the turkey, pickled radishes, sour cream and coriander.

Cream of turkey soup

A silky, soul-soothing soup that is 100 times tastier than the canned chicken version we know well.

Serves 4

1 tbsp olive oil
2 onions, sliced
3 celery sticks, sliced
2 leeks, sliced
3 garlic cloves, sliced
10g (1/3oz) chives
250ml (9fl oz) dry white wine

1 litre (1¾ pints) Turkey Stock (page 88) or chicken stock
400g (14oz) left-over turkey, ideally breast meat, torn
150ml (5¼fl oz) double (heavy) cream
salt and black pepper

Heat the oil in a large saucepan over a medium heat, then add the onions, celery and leeks with a pinch of salt. Cook for about 8 minutes until softened. Add the garlic and half the chives, and cook for 2 minutes.

Increase the heat a little and add the wine, then bubble for a few minutes to reduce a little. Stir in the stock and two-thirds of the turkey meat. Bring to the boil, then simmer gently for 30 minutes.

Remove from the heat and whizz with a stick blender until really smooth. Stir in the cream and remaining turkey. Heat through over a medium heat for about 5 minutes. Season to taste and scatter over the remaining chives to serve.

Turkey noodle salad

Fragrant with fish sauce, lime juice and chilli, plus full of fresh herbs, this Vietnamese-inspired cold noodle salad brings welcome brightness to left-over turkey.

Serves 2

2 tsp soy sauce
2½ tbsp rice vinegar
3 tsp fish sauce
200g (7oz) left-over turkey, cut into bite-sized strips
100g (3½oz) dried vermicelli rice noodles

1 carrot
½ cucumber
small handful of mint leaves
small handful of coriander (cilantro)
1 garlic clove, crushed
1 red chilli, finely chopped
juice of 1 lime

In a medium bowl, combine the soy sauce with 1 tbsp rice vinegar and 1 tsp fish sauce. Stir in the turkey and set aside while you prepare everything else.

Cook the noodles according to the pack instructions, then drain and rinse with cold water.

Coarsely grate the carrot and cut the cucumber into matchsticks. Roughly chop the herbs.

Put the garlic, chilli and lime juice in a large bowl, then stir in the remaining 1½ tbsp rice vinegar and 2 tsp fish sauce. Toss through the noodles, vegetables, herbs and the turkey with its marinade.

Turkey 'nduja turnovers

The fiery Italian pork paste 'nduja adds a spark to roast-dinner leftovers in these quick-to-pull-together puff pastry pockets.

Serves 4

1 tbsp 'nduja paste
100g (3½oz) crème fraîche
1 free-range egg, beaten
250g (9oz) left-over turkey, cut into small chunks
100g (3½oz) cooked Brussels sprouts, roughly chopped
320g (11¼oz) puff pastry sheet
salt and black pepper

Preheat the oven to 220°C (200°C fan/425°F/Gas 7).

In a large bowl, stir the 'nduja through the crème fraîche and add half the egg. Stir in the turkey and sprouts and season well.

Unroll the pastry, cut it in half lengthways and then widthways to create four rectangles.

Roasted, steamed or fried sprouts all work well here, or use any left-over cooked greens you have.

Arrange the pastry rectangles on a baking tray. Spoon one-quarter of the pie filling onto one side of each rectangle, leaving a 1-cm (½-inch) border. Brush the border with beaten egg, then fold over the pastry to encase the filling. Use a fork to seal the edges, then brush the tops with more egg.

Bake for about 20 minutes until golden.

Stuffed soda bread

With no kneading required, soda bread is quick and easy, and really delicious – especially when stuffed with shallot, cheese and left-over turkey.

Makes 1 loaf

1 banana shallot, finely chopped
2 tsp fine sea salt
400g (14oz) plain (all-purpose) flour, plus extra for dusting
1 tsp bicarbonate of soda (baking soda)
¼ tsp freshly ground black pepper
150g (5¼oz) left-over turkey, ideally dark meat, shredded into small pieces
125g (4oz) cheddar or comté, coarsely grated
300ml (10½fl oz) buttermilk

Preheat the oven to 180°C (160°C fan/350°F/ Gas 4) and dust a baking tray with flour.

Put the shallot in a bowl and stir in 1 tsp fine sea salt. Set aside for 10 minutes to help it soften.

In a large bowl, stir together the flour, bicarbonate of soda, the remaining salt and the black pepper. Stir in the turkey, onion and most of the cheese, reserving some for the top. Make a well in the centre and add the buttermilk. Mix it together with your hand in a claw shape to make a dough.

Shape the dough into a round, roughly 18cm (7 inches) in diameter and place it in the centre of the prepared baking tray. Use a sharp knife to slash the dough into quarters, without cutting all the way through. Brush the top with any scrapings left in the buttermilk pot and scatter over the reserved cheese.

Bake for 40–45 minutes until browned and the loaf sounds hollow when tapped underneath. Cool on a wire rack. This loaf is best eaten the same day.

Turkey and ham pie

*Leftovers pie is better than the main event roast in my opinion.
A creamy filling with both turkey and ham, plus plenty of veg, all
encased in flaky puff pastry – it doesn't get better.*

Serves 6

20g (¾oz) salted butter
1 tbsp olive oil
1 large onion, sliced
2 leeks, cut into slices
    about 1cm (½ inch)
    thick
2 large carrots, cut into
    slices about 1cm
    (½ inch) thick
2 parsnips, cut into
    slices about 1cm
    (½ inch) thick
3 garlic cloves, sliced
10g (⅓oz) sage leaves,
    shredded
2 tbsp plain (all-
    purpose) flour, plus
    extra for dusting

200ml (7fl oz) white
    wine
700ml (1¼ pints) Turkey
    Stock (page 88) or
    chicken stock
100g (3½oz) crème
    fraîche (heavy cream)
400g (14oz) left-over
    turkey, cut into
    chunks
200g (7oz) left-over
    roast ham, cut into
    chunks
800g (1¾lb) puff pastry
1 small free-range egg,
    beaten
salt and black pepper

*20 x 30-cm (8 x 12-inch)
    oven dish*

Recipe continues overleaf.

In a large pan, heat the butter and oil, then add the onion, leeks, carrots and parsnips with a good pinch of salt. Cook for 15 minutes until softened a little and golden in places. Stir in the garlic and sage and cook for another minute.

Add the flour and cook out for a few minutes. Add the wine, then gradually add the stock, stirring, until incorporated. Simmer for about 10 minutes, then stir in the crème fraîche and season well. Add the turkey and ham, then remove from the heat and leave to cool completely.

Once the filling is cool, preheat the oven to 210°C (190°C fan/410°F/Gas 6).

Divide the pastry into one-third and two-third pieces. Roll out the larger piece and use it to line the oven dish, leaving 2cm (¾ inch) overhanging all the way around. Scrape in the filling and brush the overhanging pastry with beaten egg.

Roll out the smaller piece of pastry until just larger than the top of the dish and sit it on top. Press the edges together and crimp. Make a few holes in the lid, then brush the top of the pastry with beaten egg.

Bake for 40–45 minutes until deep golden and bubbling.

Beetroot, turkey and cranberry grain salad

The tart sweetness of cranberry sauce is divine in a dressing with sticky balsamic vinegar over an earthy beetroot, walnut and bulgur salad.

Serves 4-6

600g (1lb 5oz) beetroot (beets), cut into 3-cm (1¼-inch) wedges
5 tbsp extra virgin olive oil
40g (1½oz) walnuts
300g (10½oz) left-over turkey, cut into strips

150g (5¼oz) bulgur wheat, freekeh or pearl barley
2 tbsp cranberry sauce
1 tbsp balsamic vinegar
½ tsp Dijon mustard
2 tsp capers
80g (2¾oz) watercress
salt and black pepper

Preheat the oven to 220°C (200°C fan/425°F/Gas 7).

Spread the beetroot out on a baking tray, drizzle with 1 tablespoon oil and season. Roast for 30–35 minutes until tender. Roast the walnuts on a separate tray for about 8 minutes, then roughly chop.

Meanwhile, get the turkey out of the fridge to come to room temperature and cook the grain of your choice according to the pack instructions.

If you're using the final scrapings of a jar of cranberry sauce to make the dressing, pop all the dressing ingredients inside, add the lid and shake it up to use every last bit.

In a jug, whisk together the remaining 4 tablespoons olive oil, the cranberry sauce, vinegar and mustard, then season.

Drain the cooked grains and tip into a bowl. Add the turkey, capers, beetroot and walnuts. Toss through the dressing followed by the watercress. Serve straight away or box up and keep in the fridge for lunches for up to 3 days.

Turkey and chorizo paella

Already-cooked turkey makes paella an easy dish for any day. Chorizo, smoked paprika and saffron give the rice a warming fragrance.

Serves 4

2 tsp olive oil
80g (2¾oz) chorizo, sliced
400-g (14-oz) can artichoke hearts, drained and halved
80g (2¾oz) frozen green beans, defrosted
pinch of saffron

1 tsp smoked paprika
1 tbsp concentrated tomato purée
250g (9oz) paella rice
1 litre hot Turkey Stock (page 88) or chicken stock
250g (9oz) left-over turkey, cut into bite-sized strips

Put the oil and chorizo in a large frying pan or paella pan and cook over a medium heat for a few minutes until the chorizo releases its oil and turns crisp. Add the artichokes and beans, then fry for a few minutes over a medium–high heat until charred. Stir in the saffron and paprika and gently fry for about 30 seconds, then stir in the tomato purée.

Stir in the rice and cook for 1 minute, then add
the stock, increase the heat and bring to the boil.
Nestle in the turkey and spread the rice evenly
in the pan. Leave to cook undisturbed for about
10 minutes over a medium–high heat.

Reduce the heat to low, without touching the
rice, cover with a lid and cook for 10–15 minutes
more until all of the stock has been absorbed.
Serve the paella dish at the centre of the table.

Turkey ragù

*Plenty of chopped veg and good-quality canned tomatoes
transform left-over turkey into a rich velvety sauce to pile onto
polenta or stir through pasta.*

Serves 2

1 tbsp olive oil
1 onion, chopped
1 small carrot, chopped
1 celery stick or 1 small
  leek, chopped
2 garlic cloves, crushed
1 tbsp concentrated
  tomato purée

100ml (3½fl oz) red
  wine
400-g (14-oz) can plum
  tomatoes
1 tsp dried oregano
200g (7oz) left-over
  turkey, cut into bite-
  sized strips
salt and black pepper

Heat the oil in a large pan over a medium heat. Add the onion,
carrot and celery with a pinch of salt and sauté for 12 minutes
until softened. Stir in the garlic and tomato purée.

Increase the heat and add the wine, then bubble until reduced
by half. Add the tomatoes, swilling out the can with a little water
and adding that too. Add the oregano and simmer gently for about
15 minutes.

Stir in the turkey and cook for 5 minutes until heated through.
Season to taste and serve.

Braised red cabbage and turkey agrodolce

The sweet-and-sour Italian condiment agrodolce combines honey, sultanas and pine nuts with vinegar and capers. It's a simple way to enhance braised red cabbage and roast turkey.

Serves 2

1 tbsp pine nuts
1 tsp olive oil
1 shallot, thinly sliced
1 red chilli, thinly sliced
2 garlic cloves, thinly sliced
2 tbsp red wine vinegar
2 tsp honey
2 tbsp sultanas (golden raisins) or raisins
1 tbsp capers
200g (7oz) left-over turkey
200g (7oz) left-over braised red cabbage
salt and black pepper

Toast the pine nuts in a dry frying pan over a medium heat for a few minutes until golden. Add the oil and, once warm, add the shallot, chilli and garlic. Cook for about 4 minutes, stirring regularly until softened. Add the vinegar, honey, sultanas and capers, then simmer for a few minutes until sticky.

Stir through the turkey and braised cabbage and cook for about 5 minutes until warmed through and combined. Season, adding more vinegar if you'd like it to be tangier, and serve with a roasted wedge of cauliflower or pile onto toast.

Shredded sprout and turkey Caesar salad

Lightly pickled Brussels sprouts and left-over turkey are a great match for crisp lettuce, garlicky croutons and an umami-rich anchovy dressing in this simple salad.

Serves 2

100g (3½oz) Brussels
 sprouts
1 tbsp white wine
 vinegar
½ tsp sugar
1 ciabatta roll
1 small garlic clove
3 tbsp mayonnaise
 (or Turkey Fat
 Mayonnaise, page 90)

4 anchovies, finely
 chopped
2 tbsp extra virgin olive
 oil, plus extra for
 drizzling
½ tsp Dijon mustard
1 head romaine lettuce
250g (9oz) roast turkey,
 cut into chunks
30g (1oz) Parmesan
salt and black pepper

Finely shred the sprouts and put in a bowl with the vinegar, sugar, a good pinch of salt and 1 tablespoon water. Set aside to pickle lightly for 30 minutes, stirring every now and then.

Halve the roll and toast it well. Cut the garlic in half, then rub it over the cut side of the toast. Cut the roll into bite-sized chunks.

Recipe continues overleaf.

With Leftovers

You can use cooked sprouts instead of raw, if you have some. No need to pickle them, just add the vinegar to the dressing.

In a large bowl, whisk together the mayonnaise, anchovies, oil and mustard. Season with salt and plenty of pepper.

Trim the base of the lettuce and separate the leaves. Add to the bowl, along with the shredded sprouts, turkey and chunks of ciabatta. Toss everything together so that it is all generously coated in the dressing.

Pile onto plates and drizzle with some more oil. Use a fine grater to cover the salads in a blanket of Parmesan.

With Leftovers

Turkey noodle soup

A cheat's take on ramen, this noodle soup uses left-over gravy to make a rich broth for noodles and slices of roast turkey.

Serves 2

2 free-range eggs
150g (5¼oz) wheat noodles
3 spring onions (scallions), sliced
2 garlic cloves, sliced
20g (¾oz) ginger, cut into matchsticks
300ml (10fl oz) left-over turkey gravy

400ml (14fl oz) Turkey Stock (page 88) or chicken stock
3 tbsp soy sauce
100g (3½oz) shiitake mushrooms
160g (5¾oz) left-over turkey, sliced
1 tsp crispy chilli oil (optional)

Boil the eggs in a pan of simmering water for 7 minutes, then use a slotted spoon to transfer to a bowl of cold water. Cook the noodles in the pan of water according to the pack instructions.

Meanwhile, put the spring onions, garlic, ginger, gravy, stock and soy sauce in a pan. Bring to the boil, then simmer for 6 minutes. Add the mushrooms and turkey, and cook for another 3 minutes.

Drain the noodles and divide between two bowls, then top with the broth. Peel the eggs and cut in half. Add to the noodle soup. Spoon over some chilli oil to serve, if desired, and season with more soy sauce, if needed.

EXTRAS

Turkey stock

Make the most of the turkey carcass and giblets with this simple stock recipe, then use it to boost the taste of so many dishes.

turkey bones (either the spine if jointed or the carcass from a roast turkey)

turkey giblets and neck (except the liver)

vegetable peelings and trimmings (onion skins, carrot ends and peelings, cabbage cores, etc) or roughly chopped celery, onion and carrot

thyme, parsley stems, bay leaves or other herbs

a few peppercorns

large pinch of fine salt

Preheat the oven to 200°C (180°C fan/400°F/Gas 6).

Roast the turkey bones and giblets for about 40 minutes (skip this if you're using the carcass of a roasted turkey).

Transfer to a large pan and add all the other ingredients. Cover with cold water, bring to the boil, then reduce the heat and simmer gently for 45 minutes. Strain the stock and discard the veg and herbs.

If you don't want to make the stock straight away, store the turkey carcass, giblets and any veg peelings and trimmings in a container in the freezer until you're ready.

You can use the stock straight away or allow it to cool and then chill for up to 1 week (or freeze for up to 6 months). If you don't have lots of freezer space, boil the strained stock to reduce the liquid by three-quarters, then freeze in small portions. Reducing it will intensify the flavour to use like a stock cube.

Turkey fat mayonnaise

Making your own mayonnaise is easier than you think and has so much more flavour – especially when made with turkey fat left over from a roast or rendered from trimmings.

Makes about 150g (5¼oz)

1 egg yolk
1 tsp Dijon mustard
125ml (4fl oz) sunflower oil

2 tbsp turkey fat (see Whipped Turkey Butter, page 95), at room temperature
1 tsp white wine vinegar or lemon juice
salt and black pepper

Put the egg yolk and mustard into a bowl, season with salt and pepper and use a balloon whisk to combine. Whisking constantly, add a small drop of oil and whisk until well combined, then add another drop and continue the process until the yolks and oil start to thicken. Once the mixture begins to combine, you can increase the amount of oil with each addition, but go slowly as too much will make the mayonnaise split.

Continue until all the oil is added and the mayo is thick. Whisk in the turkey fat and the vinegar or lemon juice. Keep in an airtight container in the fridge for up to 1 week.

Turkey gravy mayonnaise

A small amount of turkey gravy goes a long way when whisked into mayonnaise, adding a rich, roasted flavour to the condiment.

Makes about 150g (5¼oz)

1 egg yolk
1 tsp Dijon mustard
125ml (4fl oz)
 sunflower oil

50ml (1¾fl oz) cold
 turkey gravy, such as
 Roasting Tin Turkey
 Gravy (page 93)
1 tsp white wine vinegar
 or lemon juice
salt and black pepper

Put the egg yolk and mustard into a bowl, season with salt and pepper and use a balloon whisk to combine. Whisking constantly, add a small drop of oil and whisk until well combined, then add another drop and continue the process until the yolks and oil start to thicken. Once the mixture begins to combine, you can increase the amount of oil with each addition, but go slowly as too much will make the mayonnaise split.

Continue until all the oil is added and the mayo is thick. Whisk in the turkey gravy and the vinegar or lemon juice. Keep in an airtight container in the fridge for up to 5 days.

Roasting tin turkey gravy

This simple gravy recipe is all about enhancing that delectable turkey taste. It's adaptable, depending on whether you're making it alongside roasting the whole bird or using left-over bones.

whole turkey or turkey bones (uncooked wishbone and wing tips or already cooked)

turkey giblets (if not used for stock)

1 large onion (unpeeled), halved

2 carrots (unpeeled), quartered

1 celery stick or small leek

small handful thyme, rosemary, sage and/or bay leaves

olive oil, as needed

20g (¾oz) butter

3 tbsp plain (all-purpose) flour

200ml (7fl oz) white wine or dry sherry

1.3 litres (2¼ pints) Turkey Stock (page 88) or chicken stock

1 tbsp soy sauce

salt

If you're making the gravy with the tray from roasting the Whole Roast Turkey (page 15), put the onion, carrots, celery and herbs under the rack holding the bird before roasting. If not, put the turkey bones, veg, giblets and herbs in a roasting tray, drizzle with a little oil, season with salt and roast for about 40 minutes at 200°C (180°C fan/400°F/Gas 6) until golden.

Extras

You can also add vegetable peels and trimmings from your side dishes to the tray for extra flavour – onion skins, carrot ends and peelings, cabbage cores and broccoli stems all work well.

Transfer the roasting tin to the hob (after you've removed the turkey to rest) and set over a medium heat. Add the butter. Once bubbling and melted, stir in the flour and cook for a minute or two, stirring, until well toasted. Pour in the wine and bubble to reduce by half.

Stir in the stock a little at a time, stirring constantly, to combine and thicken. Once it's all added, leave to bubble for a few minutes until glossy and thickened. Stir in the soy sauce and season to taste. Strain and transfer to a serving jug.

Whipped turkey butter

Pretend you're in a fancy restaurant at home by serving up whipped turkey butter with bread to start your meal. It's very easy and a heavenly way to use up turkey fat.

Makes 120g (4oz)

30g (1oz) turkey fat
80g (2¾oz) salted
   butter

You can collect the turkey fat from the tray after roasting a whole turkey, crown or legs, or from confit legs. Or you can render the fat from pieces of raw turkey skin and fat, trimmed from the bird. To do this, put them in a small pan and melt over a medium heat until molten, then pass through a fine sieve (strainer) or muslin (cheesecloth). Leave to cool to room temperature.

Leave the butter at room temperature for an hour, so it's soft. Put the softened butter in a bowl and use a hand-held electric whisk (or a stand mixer) to whisk for about 4 minutes until really light and fluffy, then whisk in the turkey fat.

It will keep in an airtight container for up to 2 weeks in the fridge. Bring to room temperature before serving.

Turkey liver pâté

Silky smooth pâté is a sophisticated starter or snack. I've added clementine zest and orange liqueur to cut through the rich liver.

Serves 2-4

1 turkey liver, about
    100g (3½oz)
75g (2½oz) unsalted
    butter
1 small garlic clove,
    crushed

1 tbsp Grand Marnier
    or Cointreau
finely grated zest of
    1 clementine
1 bay leaf
salt

Trim any sinew from the liver. Heat 10g (⅓oz) of the butter in a large frying pan over a medium heat. Once foaming, add the liver and cook for 2 minutes on each side. Add the garlic and Grand Marnier and cook for another 2 minutes. Tip everything from the pan into a food processor with another 35g (1oz) of the butter and add the clementine zest. Whizz to a smooth paste, scraping down the sides as needed, then season with a big pinch of salt. Spoon into a ceramic dish and spread so the top is smooth.

Melt the remaining butter over a low heat, then pour it over the pâté. Add a bay leaf on top for decoration, pushing it just below the surface of the butter. Cover and chill for at least 4 hours or ideally overnight.

Take the pâté out of the fridge 30 minutes before serving. It will keep in the fridge for up to 1 week.

Marsala turkey liver pappardelle

Rich, intensely savoury liver works like a seasoning in this silky Marsala and Parmesan-coated pasta dish.

Serves 2

2 tbsp extra virgin olive oil
1 banana shallot, finely chopped
100g (3½oz) cavolo nero, shredded
2 garlic cloves, crushed
1 sprig rosemary, leaves chopped

150g (5¼oz) dried pappardelle or tagliatelle
1 turkey liver, sinew removed and finely chopped
50ml (1¾fl oz) Marsala or dry white wine
30g (1oz) salted butter
20g (¾oz) Parmesan, grated
salt and black pepper

Heat the oil in a large frying pan. Add the shallot with a pinch of salt and sauté over a medium heat for 5 minutes until soft. Stir in the cavolo nero, garlic and rosemary and cook for 5 minutes.

Meanwhile, cook the pasta in a large pan of salted boiling water for 1 minute less than the pack instructions until al dente. Drain the pasta, reserving a mugful of the cooking water.

Recipe continues overleaf.

Extras

Increase the heat to medium–high and add the turkey liver to the frying pan. Cook, stirring regularly, for 1 minute until browned. Tip in the Marsala and bubble for a few minutes.

Add the pasta to the frying pan along with the butter and Parmesan. Stir together well, splashing in some of the reserved cooking water to help it combine into a silky sauce. Season and serve.

Cheese scones with turkey fat

Adding turkey fat to cheese scones gives a wonderful flaky texture, as well as an intensely savoury taste.

Serves 8

250g (9oz) spelt flour, plus extra for dusting
1 tsp mustard powder
1½ tsp baking powder
50g (1¾oz) salted butter, cubed and chilled

50g (1¾oz) turkey fat (see Whipped Turkey Butter, page 95), cubed and chilled
75g (2½oz) mature cheddar, grated
1 free-range egg, lightly beaten
100ml (3½fl oz) milk
25g (1oz) Parmesan, grated
salt and black pepper

Put the flour in a large bowl with the mustard powder, baking powder, a pinch of salt and plenty of black pepper. Rub in the butter and turkey fat until it mostly resembles breadcrumbs, but with some larger flakes of butter and fat too. Stir in the cheddar. Add most of the egg (reserving a bit to brush the tops), followed by the milk, stirring into the mixture with a butter knife to bring it together into a dough.

Tip the dough out onto a lightly flour-dusted work surface. Roll out to 1cm (½ inch) thick, then scatter over the Parmesan. Fold the top third down and the bottom third up to create three layers of dough. Cut into eight squares. Pop on a baking tray and chill for 30 minutes.

Preheat the oven to 200°C (180°C fan/400°F/Gas 6).

Brush the top of the scones with the reserved egg. Bake for 15–18 minutes until golden. Transfer to a wire rack to cool a little, then enjoy warm. These are best eaten on the day they are made, but will keep in an airtight container for another 2 days.

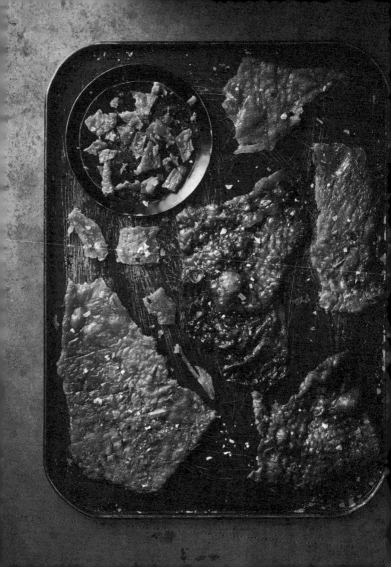

Crispy turkey skin crackling

Crispy skin is the best, so if you don't need to use the turkey skin in a dish, turn it into crackling rather than wasting it. It's a delicious snack alone or dunked into dips, it's great in a sandwich or can be crumbled up and scattered over just about anything.

turkey skin
flaky sea salt

*baking tray, lined with
   baking paper*

You could also bake these in an air fryer.

Preheat the oven to 200°C (180°C fan/400°F/Gas 6).

Place the skins upside down, flat on a board and use a small sharp knife to scrape away any attached meat or sinew, while stretching and flattening the skin, so you're left with just a thin layer.

Arrange the skins, stretched out, on the lined baking tray. Cover with another sheet of baking paper and another baking tray to hold them flat. Sit something heavy and ovenproof on top, such as a weighty pot.

Bake for about 30 minutes until crisp and golden. Sprinkle with flaky sea salt. They'll crisp up even more as they cool.

Extras

Sausagemeat and turkey liver stuffing

When you buy a whole turkey, the giblets will often be found inside a bag in the cavity of the bird. The liver is ideal for adding iron-boosting richness to this clementine and caraway stuffing.

Serves 2

2 tsp olive oil
1 tsp caraway seeds
3 shallots, finely chopped
peelings from 6–8 carrots and parsnips (or 1 large carrot), finely chopped
3 garlic cloves, chopped
finely grated zest of 1 clementine

150g (5¼oz) breadcrumbs
1 turkey liver, finely chopped
400g (14oz) outdoor-reared pork sausagemeat
salt and black pepper

900-g (2-lb) loaf tin (or similar sized baking dish)

Heat the oil in a frying pan over a medium heat, then add the caraway seeds and shallots. Cook for a few minutes until the shallots have softened, then add the veg peelings (or carrot). Cook for 5 minutes until everything has softened. Add the garlic, cook for another minute, then tip into a bowl and leave to cool.

Add the clementine zest, breadcrumbs, liver
and sausagemeat, season with a good pinch
of salt and pepper, and use your hands to mix
everything evenly. Pack into the loaf tin, then
cover with foil and chill for at least 2 hours or
overnight.

Preheat the oven to 220°C (200°C fan/425°F/
Gas 7).

Roast (still covered) for 45 minutes, then keep
warm until ready to serve.

Turn out and slice to serve.

INDEX

M

N

O

P

Published in 2024 by Murdoch Books,
an imprint of Allen & Unwin

Murdoch Books UK
Ormond House
26–27 Boswell Street
London WC1N 3JZ
Phone: +44 (0) 20 8785 5995
murdochbooks.co.uk
info@murdochbooks.co.uk

Murdoch Books Australia
Cammeraygal Country
83 Alexander Street
Crows Nest NSW 2065
Phone: +61 (0)2 8425 0100
murdochbooks.com.au
info@murdochbooks.com.au

For corporate orders and custom publishing,
contact our business development team at
salesenquiries@murdochbooks.com.au

Publisher: **Céline Hughes**
Copy-editor: **Kate Reeves-Brown**
Designer and Illustrator: **Maeve Bargman**
Photographer and Prop Stylist: **Melissa
Reynolds-James**
Food Stylist: **Emily Gussin**
Production Director: **Niccolò De Bianchi**

*Murdoch Books Australia acknowledges the
Traditional Owners of the Country on which
we live and work. We pay our respects to all
Aboriginal and Torres Strait Islander Elders,
past and present.*

ISBN 978 1 761500503

A catalogue record for this book is available
from the British Library

A catalogue record for this
book is available from the
National Library of Australia

Colour reproduction by Born Group,
London, UK
Printed by Print Best, Estonia

TABLESPOON MEASURES: We have used
15 ml (3 teaspoon) tablespoon measures.

10 9 8 7 6 5 4 3 2 1

photograph: India Whiley-Morton

About the Author

Emily Gussin is a chef, food writer and stylist based in London. She started her career in the world of cake magazines before training as a chef, completing a Cordon Bleu diploma. She has been Deputy Food Editor of *Waitrose Food* magazine and now works for *delicious.* magazine where she develops recipes, commissions contributors, styles the food and creates social videos. She also heads up the sustainability content, helping readers make ethical food choices and cut down on waste. She co-runs a seasonal supper club called 10 Miles Club for which the ingredients are sourced within 10 miles of the venue.